Pit Boss Wood Pellet Grill & Smoker Cookbook for Beginners

600-Day Tasty BBQ Recipes to Enjoy Perfect Smoking with Your Pit Boss

Seard Fobince

© Copyright 2021 Seard Fobince - All Rights Reserved.

In no way is it legal to reproduce, duplicate, or transmit any part of this document by either electronic means or in printed format. Recording of this publication is strictly prohibited, and any storage of this material is not allowed unless with written permission from the publisher. All rights reserved.

The information provided herein is stated to be truthful and consistent, in that any liability, regarding inattention or otherwise, by any usage or abuse of any policies, processes, or directions contained within is the solitary and complete responsibility of the recipient reader. Under no circumstances will any legal liability or blame be held against the publisher for any reparation, damages, or monetary loss due to the information herein, either directly or indirectly.

Respective authors own all copyrights not held by the publisher.

Legal Notice:

This book is copyright protected. This is only for personal use. You cannot amend, distribute, sell, use, quote or paraphrase any part of the content within this book without the consent of the author or copyright owner. Legal action will be pursued if this is breached.

Disclaimer Notice:

Please note the information contained within this document is for educational and entertainment purposes only. Every attempt has been made to provide accurate, up-to-date and reliable, complete information. No warranties of any kind are expressed or implied. Readers acknowledge that the author is not engaging in the rendering of legal, financial, medical or professional advice.

By reading this document, the reader agrees that under no circumstances are we responsible for any losses, direct or indirect, which are incurred as a result of the use of information contained within this document, including, but not limited to, errors, omissions, or inaccuracies.

Table of Contents

Introduction 6
Chapter 1: An Overview 7
    How Does the Pit Boss Wood Pellet Grill & Smoker Work? 7
    Tips for Cooking Success 7
    Tips for Care & Maintenance 9
    Safety Guidelines 10
Chapter 2: Chicken Recipes 12
    Garlic & Parmesan Chicken Wings 12
    Bacon-Wrapped Chicken Breast 13
    Buffalo Chicken Wings 14
    Peanut Butter & Jelly Chicken 15
    Chicken & Corn Fritters 16
    Jerk Chicken 17
    Asian Chicken Drumsticks 19
    Spicy Lime Chicken Wings 20
    Stuffed Chicken Breasts 21
    Crispy Chicken 22
Chapter 3: Fish & Seafood Recipes 23
    Cajun Shrimp 23
    Blackened Catfish 24
    Tuna Steak 25
    Shrimp with Mango Salsa 26
    Fish Tacos 27
    Grilled Lobster Tails 28
    Spicy Shrimp 29
    Honey Soy Salmon 30
    Shrimp Scampi 31
    Blackened Salmon 32

Chapter 4: Pork Recipes 33

- Chinese Barbecue Pork 33
- Maple Meatballs 34
- Maple Ham 35
- Stuffed Pork Chops 37
- Grilled Pork Tenderloin 38
- Rosemary Pork Chops 39
- Breaded Pork Chops 40
- Mustard Ribs 41
- Peppercorn Pork Chops 42
- Pulled Pork Tacos 43

Chapter 5: Beef Recipes 44

- Rib Eye Steak with Herb Butter 44
- Herbed Prime Rib Steak 46
- Beef Kefta 47
- Coffee Steak 48
- Beef Caldereta Stew 49
- Beef Shawarma 51
- Korean Barbecue Short Ribs 52
- Grilled Tomahawk Steak 53
- Steak Tips 54
- Mustard Prime Rib Roast 55

Chapter 6: Vegetable Recipes 56

- Green Chili Mashed Potatoes 56
- Cheesy Potato Casserole 58
- Garlic Potatoes 59
- Chili Verde Sauce 60
- Mexican Corn Salad 61
- Mashed Potato Cakes 62

- Grilled Cauliflower Salad 63
- Grilled Pickles with Bacon 64
- Southern Green Beans 65
- Asparagus with Bacon 66

Chapter 7: Vegetarian/Vegan Recipes 67
- Cowboy Beans 67
- Sweet Potato Casserole 68
- Sweet Potato Medley 69
- Grilled Zucchini 70
- Corn with Cilantro & Lime 71
- Tofu & Vegetable Kebab 72
- Lemon Garlic Tofu 73
- Roasted Bell Peppers 74
- Lemon Garlic Green Beans 75
- Grilled Mushrooms 76

Conclusion 77

Introduction

Grilling and smoking are two of the oldest ways to prepare food. Grilling is easy and can certainly make any food taste wonderful. It can also be a great way to enjoy the lovely outdoors or celebrate important occasions with your friends and loved ones.

Year-round grilling has also become popular especially among the millennial and Gen Z. Americans and Canadians sure love their outdoor cookers. About 64 percent of American and 72 percent of Canadian adults own a type of grill or smoker that they use regularly.

Numerous innovations provided us with options to better suit our preferences and daily needs while providing convenience. Modern grills and smokers today offer a range of options for consumers. You can choose between electric, gas, charcoal, wood pellets, briquettes, chips, or a combination of any of these to fuel your outdoor cookers.

Pellet grills have become one of the emerging favorites for customers in the last few years and for notable reasons. Apart from flavorful meals you can easily make with pellet grills, they are excellent cookers that can perform numerous functions like grill, smoke, bake, sear, braise, and roast. Pellet grills are easy to use, fuel-efficient, and sometimes even have smart controls and wireless capabilities.

The Pit Boss brand was first established in Canada back in 1999. Today, they feature a vast number of grills, smokers, combination type grills, as well as various grilling equipment and accessories. Learn more about one of the most popular brands in the grilling world and discover gratifying recipes you can try with a pellet grill.

Chapter 1: An Overview

How Does the Pit Boss Wood Pellet Grill & Smoker Work?

Wood pellet grills are outdoor cookers that blend the functions of a gas/charcoal grill, convection oven, and smoker into one awesome appliance. Pellet grills, or sometimes called pellet smokers, operate similarly regardless of the brand or make. The grill will have to be first plugged into a grounded power source.

A hopper, which is a lidded container located on one side of the grill, is then filled with your choice of wood pellets. When the grill is powered on, a rotating cylindrical screw called an auger, will then begin to slowly feed wood pellets into the fire pot. The fire pot has an igniter that burns the pellets. The grill will then start to heat up with the help of combustion fans.

Intake fans will help disperse the heat and smoke inside the cooking barrel until it reaches the temperature that you have set. Pit Boss wood pellet grills have a temperature range of 180 degrees Fahrenheit to 500 degrees Fahrenheit. Letting you smoke meats at low temperatures and sear at high temperatures.

Tips for Cooking Success

Cooking with the Pit Boss pellet grill is simple and will give you mouth-watering dishes that everyone will love. To make sure that you get the best results each time you cook, remember these useful tips.

- Thoroughly wash your hands with warm water and soap before any food preparation.
- Organize everything you need before grilling. This involves studying the recipe beforehand and preparing all needed ingredients and utensils.
- Avoid cross contamination by using separate utensils for raw and cooked meat.
- To get a more delectable result, cook low and slow. Cooking food at lower

temperatures for longer will help keep the smoky flavors in. Just remember to baste or mist the surface to maintain the juices and avoid drying.

- When cooking meat, it is best to rely on internal temperature rather than the time indicated in a recipe. Refer to the manual's Cooking Guidelines or to the Safe Minimum Internal Temperature Chart by the USDA.
- You can cook meat that came straight out of the fridge. Do not let meat come down to room temperature before cooking.
- Never overcrowd the grill unless you are okay with an extended cooking time.
- To avoid flare ups, use thick, sweet sauces towards the end of the grilling session.
- If the food keeps sticking to the grill, use an oil-soaked paper towel or half an onion and wipe the grill surface using a long-handled tong.
- Use oils with a high smoking point like canola, coconut, and peanut.
- Use your pellet smoker as you would an oven. The added smoky character to baked goods makes them extra special.
- If your grill has more than one rack, you can use the upper rack to cook foods with convection rather than direct heat. The upper rack is perfect for cooking briskets evenly and for foods that tend to dry out. Put a pan of water on the bottom rack for best results.
- Learn about the different cuts of meat to get a better grasp of how each should be cooked. Leaner meats will most likely dry out quickly while too much fat can cause a grease fire and can make it harder for the smoky taste to penetrate the interior.
- If you plan on smoking some ribs, you should never skip removing the membrane. When smoked, this can become very rubber-like which makes it harder to eat.
- Make sure there are adequate pellets in the hopper, especially for recipes that require a longer time to cook. Setting a timer on your phone can help you be reminded if you need to re-load the hopper.
- Allow the meat to rest for a few minutes before serving.
- If you have not tried it already, learn how to reverse sear. This process involves cooking the meat at low temperatures first, then finishing with a high temperature

to sear the exteriors. The reverse sear is an excellent way to cook thicker cuts of meat or poultry.
- You can experiment with different wood pellet flavors to add magnificent dimensions to any dish. Pit Boss has a wide range of pellet blends that goes well with your favorite foods. Competition blend is a perfect all-around seasoning that can be used with any meat as well as fruits and vegetables. Hickory is wonderful for smoking meats. Apple has a nice and pleasant flavor ideal for baking in your pellet grill. Recently, Pit Boss released their charcoal flavored pellets that go well with beef, pork, poultry, wild game, and even pizza.

Tips for Care & Maintenance

Sufficient care and maintenance are at the core of prolonging the life and service of your beloved pellet grill. Make sure to follow these helpful tips to keep your grills in an excellent working condition.

- Follow the priming, burn-off, and start-up process indicated in the instruction manual. Priming the hopper is done if you are using the grill for the very first time. Burn-off is also done before you use the grill for the first time and in between cooking sessions.
- Clean the fire pot, cooking chamber, and grease bucket regularly. A build up of ash in the fire pot will make it hard for the igniter to start combusting.
- Inspect the fire pot and auger for any obstruction or debris before firing up the grill.
- Lining the grease bucket with foil will make clean-up much easier.
- Use a vacuum to clean the ash in the nooks and crannies inside the cooking barrel.
- Pit Boss recommends that your wood pellet grill should be cleaned every after you finish a bag of pellets.
- The best time to clean the cooking grates is after a cooking session while it is still warm. Use a cleaning brush to remove any debris inside the cooking barrel.

- Using a clean cloth and soapy water, wipe the exterior and removable parts after each use to prevent build-up of gunk.
- Never use abrasive chemicals and oven cleaners on the exterior to avoid damaging the coating.
- The user's manual provides detailed information on how often each part should be cleaned and what cleaning method to use.
- Keep wood pellets in a lidded container in a cool, dry place. Always examine the pellets before putting them in the hopper. Moist or wet wood pellets have a potential to damage or clog the auger.
- Remove leftover pellets from the auger and hopper if you will not be using the grill for an extended period.
- Avoid folding the temperature probe wire tightly as this may cause damage. Store the wire loosely and keep them away from water. A damaged probe should be immediately replaced as this will provide inaccurate readings.
- Keep the barrel closed when not in use. If you need to store the grill over a long period of time, using a grill cover and leaving your grill in the garage will protect it from the elements.

Safety Guidelines

Reviewing the instruction manual for your Pit Boss wood pellet grill should be done before any operation. The manual will also help you be familiar with the different parts, get an idea on what function they serve, and where to locate them. Here are some of the important safety guidelines to keep in mind.

- Wood pellet grills are intended to be used outdoors at least 6 feet away from any structure. Ensure that you have a clearance of at least 12 inches around the grill.
- Only use the grill in a well-ventilated area.
- Always exercise caution when using the appliance as surfaces can become heated. Keep children and pets away from the grill while it is in use.

- Always make sure that the grill has completely cooled down and unplugged before conducting any cleaning and maintenance.
- Inspect the electrical cords for any signs of wear and tear before plugging in to a power source. Contact a professional and do not use the appliance if there are visible signs of damage or if the appliance is malfunctioning.
- Keep all combustible materials away from the grill. This includes combustible floors and ceilings, as well as combustible covers for said areas. Similarly, highly flammable vapors, fuels, and liquids should be placed far away from the grill.
- Grease from fatty food can cause flare-ups. Immediately close the lid to put out the fire if this happens. If unsuccessful, carefully remove the food and unplug the grill.
- Never use water to put out a grease fire. Sprinkle some baking soda or salt over the grill or if the fire gets too hard to handle, reach for the fire extinguisher.
- Protect the electrical cords from water, moisture, and heated surfaces.
- Never operate the grill during inclement weather or near a body of water. For safety reasons and to ensure that the wood pellets remain dry while in operation, never use the grill or smoker in the rain.
- Keep an all-class fire extinguisher at hand for additional safety.
- Never move or transfer the pellet grill while in use or while it is still hot.
- Do not modify any of the parts to ensure optimum safety and to keep your warranty.
- Use only good quality and food-grade pellets. Pellets made from hardwood give a longer and steadier burn.
- Pellet grills are also awesome smokers and are often equipped with monitoring systems to help you keep track of the long smoking process. While it is great that these cookers can do most of the cooking for you, it is best practice to always check on your grill and not leave it unattended for extended periods while it is on.

Chapter 2: Chicken Recipes

Garlic & Parmesan Chicken Wings

Preparation Time: 15 minutes
Cooking Time: 25 minutes
Servings: 4

Ingredients:

- 4 lb. chicken wings
- Pinch chicken seasoning
- 2 tablespoons olive oil
- 4 tablespoons butter
- 4 cloves garlic, minced
- 2 tablespoons parsley, chopped
- ½ cup Parmesan cheese, shredded

Method:

1. Season the chicken wings with chicken seasoning.
2. Preheat the Pit Boss grill to 400 degrees F or to medium high heat.
3. Grill the chicken wings for 20 minutes, turning 3 to 5 times.
4. In a pan over medium heat, add the olive oil and butter.
5. Cook the garlic for 30 seconds.
6. Toss the chicken wings in the garlic butter sauce.
7. Sprinkle with the parsley and Parmesan cheese and serve.

Serving Suggestions: Serve with tartar sauce or hot sauce.

Preparation & Cooking Tips: Brush the chicken wings with coconut oil first before grilling to get crispier results.

Bacon-Wrapped Chicken Breast

Preparation Time: 10 minutes
Cooking Time: 30 minutes
Servings: 4

Ingredients:

- 4 chicken breast fillet
- 1 tablespoon olive oil
- 2 teaspoons garlic salt
- 1 teaspoon dried rosemary
- 8 slices bacon
- 1 tablespoon butter

Method:

1. Preheat your Pit Boss grill to 375 degrees F or to medium heat.
2. Brush both sides of chicken with olive oil.
3. Sprinkle with the garlic salt and rosemary.
4. Wrap 2 bacon slices per chicken breast fillet.
5. Brush with butter.
6. Place on the grill.
7. Grill for 30 minutes, turning every 5 minutes.

Serving Suggestions: Garnish with chopped parsley.

Preparation & Cooking Tips: You can also use chicken seasoning in place of garlic salt.

Buffalo Chicken Wings

Preparation Time: 10 minutes
Cooking Time: 25 minutes
Servings: 4

Ingredients:

- 2 lb. chicken wings
- ½ cup Pit Boss sweet heat rub
- ½ cup buffalo sauce

Method:

1. Preheat your Pit Boss grill to 450 degrees F or to high heat.
2. Season chicken with the rub.
3. Place on the grill.
4. Cook for 20 minutes, flipping halfway through.
5. Brush with the buffalo sauce.
6. Cook for another 7 to 10 minutes.
7. Dip in remaining buffalo sauce before serving.

Serving Suggestions: Serve with celery and blue cheese dip.

Preparation & Cooking Tips: For crispier chicken wings, try grilling while frozen.

Peanut Butter & Jelly Chicken

Preparation Time: 2 hours and 15 minutes
Cooking Time: 35 minutes
Servings: 4

Ingredients:

Sauce

- ¼ cup peanut butter
- 1 tablespoon chili sauce
- 2 tablespoons honey
- ½ cup strawberry preserves
- ¼ cup Worcestershire sauce
- 2 tablespoons brown sugar
- ½ red onion, chopped
- 1 teaspoon black pepper

Chicken

- 4 lb. chicken thigh or chicken wings

Method:

1. Combine sauce ingredients in a bowl.
2. Transfer half to another bowl.
3. Add the chicken to one of the bowls.
4. Cover and refrigerate for 2 hours.
5. Preheat your Pit Boss Grill to 400 degrees F or medium high heat.
6. Grill the chicken for 25 to 30 minutes, turning every 5 minutes.
7. Soak the chicken in the reserved sauce before serving.

Serving Suggestions: Serve with additional chili sauce.

Preparation & Cooking Tips: Use natural organic peanut butter for best results.

Chicken & Corn Fritters

Preparation Time: 15 minutes

Cooking Time: 45 minutes

Servings: 8

Ingredients:

- 1 ½ lb. ground chicken
- 1 cup cheddar cheese, shredded
- 2 eggs, beaten
- ¾ cup corn kernels
- 2 teaspoons baking powder
- ¾ cup flour

Method:

1. Preheat your Pit Boss Grill to 425 degrees F or medium high heat.
2. Combine all the ingredients in a bowl.
3. Form patties from the mixture.
4. Add the patties to the grill.
5. Cook for 20 minutes, flipping every 5 minutes.

Serving Suggestions: Serve with sour cream.

Preparation & Cooking Tips: You can use leftover chicken for this recipe.

Jerk Chicken

Preparation Time: 2 hours and 15 minutes
Cooking Time: 20 minutes
Servings: 10

Ingredients:

- 1 teaspoon ground allspice
- ½ teaspoon ground nutmeg
- ½ teaspoon ground cinnamon
- 2 teaspoons dried thyme
- 4 cloves garlic, minced
- 2 teaspoons ginger, grated
- 1 Habanero pepper, chopped
- ¼ cup Poblano pepper, minced
- ½ cup yellow onion, minced
- ½ cup olive oil
- 2 tablespoons lemon juice
- 1/3 cup lime juice
- 2 tablespoons honey
- 1 tablespoon tamari
- 3 lb. chicken wings

Method:

1. Combine all the ingredients except chicken in a food processor.
2. Process until smooth.
3. Transfer to a bowl.
4. Stir in chicken.
5. Cover and refrigerate for 2 hours.

6. Preheat your Pit Boss Grill to 425 degrees F or medium high heat.
7. Grill chicken for 20 minutes, flipping every 5 minutes.

Serving Suggestions: Serve warm.

Preparation & Cooking Tips: To ensure even cooking, move the chicken closer to the heat each time you flip it.

Asian Chicken Drumsticks

Preparation Time: 30 minutes
Cooking Time: 45 minutes
Servings: 3

Ingredients:

- 3 lb. chicken drumsticks
- 2 teaspoons sesame oil
- 2 cloves garlic, minced
- 2 teaspoons ginger, grated
- ¼ cup brown sugar
- 2 tablespoons honey

Method:

1. Set your Pit Boss Grill to smoke mode.
2. Preheat it to 350 degrees F or to medium heat.
3. Grill the chicken drumsticks over indirect heat for 30 minutes, flipping every 5 minutes.
4. Transfer chicken to a plate.
5. Add the sesame oil to a pan over medium heat.
6. Cook the garlic and ginger for 30 seconds.
7. Stir in the sugar and honey.
8. Cook for 3 minutes, stirring.
9. Dip the chicken in the sauce and serve.

Serving Suggestions: Garnish with chopped scallions and sesame seeds. Serve with chili sauce.

Preparation & Cooking Tips: Dry chicken thoroughly before seasoning.

Spicy Lime Chicken Wings

Preparation Time: 1 hour and 10 minutes
Cooking Time: 20 minutes
Servings: 4

Ingredients:

- 1 teaspoon chili powder
- 2 lb. chicken wings
- 2 tablespoons cilantro, chopped
- 1 teaspoon cumin
- 1 lime zest
- 1 ½ tablespoons olive oil

Method:

1. Combine all the ingredients in a bowl.
2. Cover and refrigerate for 1 hour.
3. Preheat your Pit Boss Grill to 350 degrees F or to medium heat.
4. Grill the chicken wings for 15 to 20 minutes, flipping every 5 minutes.

Serving Suggestions: Garnish with chopped parsley.

Preparation & Cooking Tips: You can also use chicken thighs for this recipe.

Stuffed Chicken Breasts

Preparation Time: 15 minutes
Cooking Time: 35 minutes
Servings: 4

Ingredients:

- 4 chicken breast fillets
- 3 cloves garlic, minced
- 8 oz. Italian sausage, crumbled and cooked
- 8 oz. ricotta cheese
- 8 oz. mozzarella cheese, sliced
- 2 tablespoons Italian parsley, minced

Method:

1. Set your Pit Boss Grill to smoke mode.
2. Preheat it to 400 degrees F or medium high heat for 10 minutes.
3. Flatten the chicken with a meat mallet.
4. Mix the rest of the ingredients in a bowl.
5. Top the chicken with the mixture and roll.
6. Secure with a toothpick.
7. Add the chicken to the grill.
8. Cook for 35 minutes, flipping 4 times.

Serving Suggestions: Garnish with chopped fresh basil.

Preparation & Cooking Tips: You can also slice a pocket in the chicken breast.

Crispy Chicken

Preparation Time: 10 minutes
Cooking Time: 50 minutes
Servings: 6

Ingredients:

- 1 cup cornmeal
- 1 cup flour
- 2 tablespoons chicken seasoning
- 2 eggs, beaten
- 1 cup milk
- 4 lb. chicken

Method:

1. Preheat your Pit Boss Grill to 300 degrees F for medium low heat.
2. In a bowl, mix the cornmeal, flour and chicken seasoning.
3. In another bowl, combine the eggs and milk.
4. Dip the chicken in the eggs and then dredge with flour.
5. Add to the grill.
6. Cook for 50 minutes, flipping every 10 minutes.

Serving Suggestions: Let rest for 10 minutes before serving.

Preparation & Cooking Tips: You can also season the chicken first with chicken seasoning before coating with flour.

Chapter 3: Fish & Seafood Recipes

Cajun Shrimp

Preparation Time: 10 minutes
Cooking Time: 15 minutes
Servings: 4

Ingredients:

- 2 tablespoons olive oil
- ½ lb. shrimp, peeled and deveined
- 1 tablespoon Cajun seasoning

Cajun Dip

- ½ cup mayonnaise
- 1 cup sour cream
- 1 teaspoon Cajun seasoning
- 1 clove garlic, minced
- 1 teaspoon lemon juice
- 1 tablespoon hot sauce

Method:

1. Preheat your Pit Boss Grill to 350 degrees F or medium heat.
2. Brush shrimp with olive oil.
3. Season with the Cajun seasoning.
4. Grill for 15 minutes, turning every 5 minutes.
5. Mix the dip ingredients in a bowl.
6. Serve shrimp with dip.

Serving Suggestions: Sprinkle with chopped chives.

Preparation & Cooking Tips: Use fresh shrimp instead of frozen for this recipe.

Blackened Catfish

Preparation Time: 30 minutes

Cooking Time: 10 minutes

Servings: 4

Ingredients:

- ½ cup Cajun seasoning
- 1 teaspoon garlic, grated
- ¼ teaspoon cayenne pepper
- 1 teaspoon onion powder
- 1 teaspoon ground thyme
- 1 teaspoon pepper
- 1 teaspoon ground oregano
- 1 tablespoon smoked paprika
- 4 catfish fillets
- ½ cup butter

Method:

1. Combine all the seasoning and spices in a bowl.
2. Sprinkle the fish with the spice mixture.
3. Marinate for 20 minutes.
4. Preheat your Pit Boss Grill to 450 degrees F or medium high heat.
5. Add a cast iron pan on the grill.
6. Add the butter.
7. Cook the fish in the pan for 5 minutes per side.

Serving Suggestions: Garnish with lemon wedges.

Preparation & Cooking Tips: You can also smoke the fish before grilling it.

Tuna Steak

Preparation Time: 1 hour and 10 minutes
Cooking Time: 20 minutes
Servings: 2

Ingredients:

- 2 tuna steaks
- Salt and pepper to taste
- ¼ cup lime juice
- 2 tablespoons rice wine vinegar
- 2 tablespoons sesame oil
- ½ cup soy sauce

Method:

1. Preheat your Pit Boss Grill to 400 degrees F or to high heat.
2. Season the tuna with salt and pepper.
3. Mix the remaining ingredients in a bowl.
4. Add the tuna to the bowl.
5. Cover and marinate in the refrigerator for 1 hour.
6. Add to the grill.
7. Cook for 45 minutes, turning every 15 minutes.

Serving Suggestions: Serve with wasabi mayo dip.

Preparation & Cooking Tips: You can also use other fish fillet for this recipe.

Shrimp with Mango Salsa

Preparation Time: 15 minutes
Cooking Time: 6 minutes
Servings: 4

Ingredients:

- 2 lb. shrimp, peeled and deveined
- 1 teaspoon olive oil
- Salt and pepper to taste

Salsa

- 2 cups mango, chopped
- ¼ cup cucumber, chopped
- ½ red onion, minced
- 1 teaspoon lemon juice
- 1 tablespoon parsley, chopped

Method:

1. Preheat your Pit Boss Grill to 425 degrees F.
2. Thread the shrimp onto skewers.
3. Brush with oil.
4. Season with salt and pepper.
5. Grill for 3 minutes per side.
6. Mix salsa ingredients in a bowl.
7. Serve shrimp with salsa.

Serving Suggestions: Sprinkle shrimp with chopped chives.

Preparation & Cooking Tips: Soak wooden skewers in water before using.

Fish Tacos

Preparation Time: 10 minutes

Cooking Time: 6 minutes

Servings: 12

Ingredients:

- 1 teaspoon garlic powder
- 1 teaspoon oregano
- 1 teaspoon black pepper
- ½ teaspoon cumin
- ¼ teaspoon cayenne pepper
- 1 ½ teaspoon paprika
- 1 ½ lb. cod fish

For assembling

- Tortillas
- Chopped lettuce
- Sour cream

Method:

1. Preheat your Pit Boss Grill to 350 degrees F.
2. Mix the spices in a bowl.
3. Sprinkle fish with the spice mixture.
4. Grill for 3 minutes per side.
5. Top the tortillas with the fish, lettuce and sour cream.

Serving Suggestions: Serve with tomato salsa.

Preparation & Cooking Tips: Toast the tortillas first before topping with the fish.

Grilled Lobster Tails

Preparation Time: 10 minutes
Cooking Time: 10 minutes
Servings: 3

Ingredients:

- ¾ stick butter, softened
- 1 clove garlic, minced
- 2 tablespoons chives, chopped
- Salt and pepper to taste
- 3 lobster tails, butterflied

Method:

1. Set your Pit Boss to smoke.
2. Preheat your grill to 350 degrees F.
3. In a bowl, mix the butter, garlic, chives, salt and pepper.
4. Brush the lobster tails with the butter mixture.
5. Grill for 5 minutes per side.

Serving Suggestions: Pair with grilled steak for a "surf and turf" dinner.

Preparation & Cooking Tips: Use maple blend wood pellets for this recipe.

Spicy Shrimp

Preparation Time: 40 minutes
Cooking Time: 6 minutes
Servings: 4

Ingredients:

- 2 cloves garlic, minced
- 2 teaspoons chili paste
- ½ teaspoon cumin
- 1 tablespoon lime juice
- ¼ teaspoon paprika
- ¼ teaspoon red pepper flakes
- 1 lb. shrimp, peeled and deveined

Method:

1. Combine all the ingredients except shrimp in a bowl.
2. Mix well.
3. Stir in the shrimp and coat evenly with mixture.
4. Cover and marinate for 30 minutes.
5. Thread shrimp onto skewers.
6. Preheat your Pit Boss to 400 degrees F.
7. Add the shrimp to the grill.
8. Grill for 3 minutes per side.

Serving Suggestions: Garnish with lime wedges.

Preparation & Cooking Tips: Thaw shrimp before seasoning if using frozen.

Honey Soy Salmon

Preparation Time: 45 minutes
Cooking Time: 6 minutes
Servings: 4

Ingredients:

- 1 teaspoon sesame oil
- 1 teaspoon chili paste
- 2 tablespoons ginger, minced
- 2 cloves garlic, grated
- 2 tablespoons lemon, juice
- 1 teaspoon honey
- 2 tablespoons soy sauce
- 4 salmon fillets

Method:

1. Set your Pit Boss Grill to smoke.
2. Preheat it to 400 degrees F.
3. Add all ingredients except salmon to a bowl.
4. Mix well.
5. Add the salmon and coat evenly with marinade.
6. Refrigerate for 30 minutes.
7. Grill the salmon for 3 minutes per side.

Serving Suggestions: Garnish with chopped chives.

Preparation & Cooking Tips: You can marinate longer for 4 hours.

Shrimp Scampi

Preparation Time: 15 minutes
Cooking Time: 10 minutes
Servings: 3

Ingredients:

- ½ cup butter, sliced into cubes
- 3 cloves garlic, minced
- 2 teaspoons blackened rub seasoning
- ½ teaspoon red pepper flakes
- 1 ½ lb. shrimp, peeled and deveined
- 1 tablespoon lemon juice
- 1 teaspoon lemon zest
- 3 tablespoons parsley, chopped

Method:

1. Preheat your Pit Boss Grill to medium high.
2. Add a pan on top of the grill.
3. Add the butter.
4. Cook the garlic until fragrant.
5. Stir in the blackened rub seasoning and red pepper flakes.
6. Stir in the shrimp and cook for 2 minutes, stirring.
7. Mix the remaining ingredients in a bowl and add to the pan.
8. Simmer for 5 minutes and serve.

Serving Suggestions: Serve on top of pasta or with toasted baguette.

Preparation & Cooking Tips: You can also serve this with zucchini noodles.

Blackened Salmon

Preparation Time: 15 minutes
Cooking Time: 10 minutes
Servings: 4

Ingredients:

- 2 lb. salmon fillets
- 2 tablespoons olive oil
- 1 tablespoon cayenne pepper
- 4 tablespoons sweet rib rub
- 2 cloves garlic, minced

Method:

1. Preheat your Pit Boss Grill to 350 degrees F.
2. Brush both sides of the salmon with olive oil.
3. Sprinkle with cayenne pepper, sweet rib rub and minced garlic.
4. Grill the fish for 5 minutes per side.

Serving Suggestions: Top with crispy garlic bits before serving.

Preparation & Cooking Tips: Use New England apple fruit hardwood pellets for this recipe.

Chapter 4: Pork Recipes

Chinese Barbecue Pork

Preparation Time: 4 hours and 10 minutes
Cooking Time: 20 minutes
Servings: 4

Ingredients:

- ¼ cup hoisin sauce
- 2 cloves garlic, minced
- ¼ cup barbecue sauce
- 1 tablespoon sugar
- 1 teaspoon sweet rib rub seasoning
- ¼ cup tamari
- ¼ cup white wine
- 2 lb. pork tenderloin, fat trimmed

Method:

1. Combine all the ingredients except pork in a bowl.
2. Mix well.
3. Stir in the pork.
4. Cover and refrigerate for 4 hours.
5. Set your Pit Boss Grill to smoke.
6. Preheat it to 400 degrees F or medium high heat.
7. Add the pork on the grill.
8. Cook for 5 minutes per side.
9. Brush with the marinade.
10. Cook for another 5 minutes per side.

Serving Suggestions: Pair with sautéed garlic green beans.

Preparation & Cooking Tips: Internal temperature should be at least 145 degrees F.

Maple Meatballs

Preparation Time: 15 minutes
Cooking Time: 15 minutes
Servings: 4

Ingredients:

- 2 lb. ground pork
- 1 onion, grated
- 3 cloves garlic, minced
- 2 eggs, beaten
- 1 tablespoon maple syrup
- 1 tablespoon sweet heat rub
- 2 tablespoons milk

Method:

1. Preheat your Pit Boss grill to 350 degrees F or to medium heat.
2. Combine all the ingredients in a bowl.
3. Form meatballs from the mixture.
4. Add the meatballs to the grill.
5. Cook for 15 minutes, turning three times.

Serving Suggestions: Serve with hot sauce and mustard.

Preparation & Cooking Tips: You can also use a combination of ground beef and ground pork.

Maple Ham

Preparation Time: 30 minutes
Cooking Time: 3 hours
Servings: 12

Ingredients:

Glaze

- 3 tablespoons apple cider vinegar
- 1 ½ cups apple cider
- 2 tablespoons butter
- ½ cup brown sugar
- ½ cup maple syrup
- ¼ teaspoons chili powder
- 3 tablespoons Dijon mustard
- 2 teaspoons cornstarch
- ¼ teaspoon ground cloves
- ½ teaspoon ground cinnamon
- ¼ teaspoon dried thyme
- 2 teaspoon apple butter rub
- 3 tablespoons mustard

Ham

- 1 whole ham
- 1 cup water

Method:

1. Preheat your Pit Boss Grill to 400 degrees F.
2. Add a cast iron pan to your grill.

3. Combine the glaze ingredients in the pan.
4. Mix well.
5. Bring to a boil.
6. Reduce grill temperature to 300 degrees F.
7. Simmer for 20 minutes, stirring every 5 to 6 minutes.
8. Remove from the grill and set aside.
9. Add the ham to a baking pan.
10. Pour in the water and 1/3 of the glaze.
11. Cook for 2 hours.
12. Brush the ham with the glaze.
13. Grill for another 30 minutes or until caramelized.
14. Brush with the remaining glaze.
15. Grill for another 15 minutes.

Serving Suggestions: Let rest for 15 minutes before slicing and serving.

Preparation & Cooking Tips: Let ham rest at room temperature for 30 minutes before cooking.

Stuffed Pork Chops

Preparation Time: 30 minutes
Cooking Time: 30 minutes
Servings: 4

Ingredients:

- 4 pork chops
- Pinch pulled pork seasoning
- 1 tablespoons parsley, chopped
- 1 white onion, chopped
- 1 pack hash browns, shredded
- ¼ cup sour cream
- 1 cup cheddar cheese, shredded

Method:

1. Slice a pocket in the middle of the pork chops.
2. Sprinkle both sides of the pork chops with the seasoning.
3. In a bowl, mix the rest of the ingredients.
4. Stuff the pork chops with the mixture.
5. Preheat your Pit Boss Grill to 350 degrees F or medium heat.
6. Grill the pork chops for 30 minutes, flipping halfway through.

Serving Suggestions: Sprinkle with pepper before serving.

Preparation & Cooking Tips: You can also marinate overnight for more intense flavors.

Grilled Pork Tenderloin

Preparation Time: 1 hour and 10 minutes
Cooking Time: 10 minutes
Servings: 4

Ingredients:

- 2 tablespoons olive oil
- 2 tablespoons brown sugar
- 2 tablespoons apple butter seasoning
- 1 pork tenderloin, fat trimmed

Method:

1. Mix the olive oil, sugar and apple butter seasoning in a bowl.
2. Rub all sides of the pork tenderloin with the mixture.
3. Cover and marinate for 1 hour.
4. Set your Pit Boss Grill to smoke.
5. Preheat it to 350 degrees F.
6. Grill the pork for 5 minutes per side.

Serving Suggestions: Let rest for 10 minutes before slicing and serving.

Preparation & Cooking Tips: Internal temperature should reach 145 degrees F.

Rosemary Pork Chops

Preparation Time: 3 hours and 15 minutes

Cooking Time: 10 minutes

Servings: 4

Ingredients:

- 1 cup soy sauce
- 6 tablespoons brown sugar
- 2 tablespoons dried rosemary
- ½ cup water
- 4 pork chops

Method:

1. Combine soy sauce, brown sugar, rosemary and water in a bowl.
2. Add the pork chops and coat evenly with the sauce.
3. Cover and marinate for 3 hours.
4. Set your Pit Boss Grill to smoke.
5. Preheat it to 350 degrees F.
6. Grill the pork chops for 5 minutes per side.

Serving Suggestions: Let rest for 10 minutes before serving.

Preparation & Cooking Tips: Oil the grates before adding the pork chops.

Breaded Pork Chops

Preparation Time: 20 minutes

Cooking Time: 6 minutes

Servings: 6

Ingredients:

- 6 pork chops
- Salt and pepper to taste
- 1 teaspoon dried rosemary
- ½ cup flour
- 1 ½ cup breadcrumbs
- ½ cup vegetable oil

Method:

1. Season pork chops with salt and pepper.
2. Sprinkle with dried rosemary.
3. Coat with flour.
4. Dip in egg and dredge with breadcrumbs.
5. Add the oil to a pan.
6. Place the pan on top of the Pit Boss Grill.
7. Set the Pit Boss Grill to medium heat.
8. Cook the pork chops for 3 minutes per side or until golden.

Serving Suggestions: Serve with sour cream mixed with mustard.

Preparation & Cooking Tips: Dry the pork chops thoroughly before seasoning.

Mustard Ribs

Preparation Time: 20 minutes
Cooking Time: 6 hours
Servings: 4

Ingredients:

- 2 cups yellow mustard
- 2 cups apple juice
- ¼ cup cider vinegar
- ¼ cup honey
- ¼ cup brown sugar
- 2 tablespoons ketchup
- 1 tablespoon hot sauce
- 1 tablespoon Worcestershire sauce
- 7 tablespoon sweet rib rub
- 1 rack ribs

Method:

1. Combine all the ingredients except the ribs.
2. Mix well.
3. Coat ribs with the mixture.
4. Preheat your Pit Boss Grill to 275 degrees F.
5. Add the ribs to the grill.
6. Grill for 3 hours, turning every 1 hour.
7. Brush with the sauce.
8. Grill for another 3 hours, flipping every 1 hour.

Serving Suggestions: Serve immediately.

Preparation & Cooking Tips: You can add more hot sauce if you like the ribs spicier.

Peppercorn Pork Chops

Preparation Time: 15 minutes
Cooking Time: 15 minutes
Servings: 4

Ingredients:

- 4 pork chops
- 1 teaspoon olive oil
- 1 tablespoon coriander
- 3 tablespoons peppercorns, ground
- 2 tablespoons sugar
- ¼ cup cumin
- 1 teaspoon dry rub
- Salt to taste

Method:

1. Preheat your Pit Boss Grill to 450 degrees F.
2. Brush pork chops with olive oil.
3. Mix the remaining ingredients in a bowl.
4. Sprinkle both sides of pork chops with this mixture.
5. Grill the pork chops for 5 to 7 minutes per side.

Serving Suggestions: Serve with grilled corn.

Preparation & Cooking Tips: Use bone-in pork chops for this recipe.

Pulled Pork Tacos

Preparation Time: 15 minutes

Cooking Time: 5 minutes

Servings: 4

Ingredients:

- 4 tortillas
- 2 cups cooked pulled pork
- ½ cup radish, sliced into strips
- 1 white onion, chopped
- ¼ cup cucumber, chopped
- Chopped cilantro

Method:

1. Preheat your Pit Boss grill to 350 degrees F.
2. Top the tortillas with all the ingredients.
3. Fold and place on the grill.
4. Grill for 1 to 2 minutes per side.

Serving Suggestions: Drizzle with lime juice before serving.

Preparation & Cooking Tips: Use either corn or flour tortillas.

Chapter 5: Beef Recipes

Rib Eye Steak with Herb Butter

Preparation Time: 1 day and 10 minutes
Cooking Time: 1 hour
Servings: 2

Ingredients:

Herb butter

- ¼ cup butter
- 1 teaspoon horseradish
- 1 tablespoon parsley, chopped

Marinade

- ¼ cup olive oil
- 2 cloves garlic, minced
- ¼ cup red wine
- 2 teaspoon pepper
- 1 tablespoon Dijon mustard
- 1 tablespoon red wine vinegar
- 1 tablespoon dried rosemary
- 1 teaspoon Worcestershire sauce

Steak

- 2 rib eye steaks

Method:

1. Mix the herb butter ingredients in a small bowl.
2. Cover and refrigerate.

3. Combine the marinade ingredients in a sealable plastic bag.
4. Add the steaks and turn to coat evenly.
5. Marinate in the refrigerator overnight.
6. Set your Pit Boss Grill to smoke.
7. Preheat your grill to 350 degrees F.
8. Add the steaks to the grill.
9. Smoke for 40 to 50 minutes.
10. Increase temperature to 375 degrees F.
11. Grill the steaks for 15 minutes.
12. Add the herb butter on top and serve.

Serving Suggestions: Let rest for 10 minutes before serving.

Preparation & Cooking Tips: Internal temperatures of steak: 125 degrees F for rare, 130 degrees F for medium-rare, 140 degrees F for medium, 160 degrees F for well done.

Herbed Prime Rib Steak

Preparation Time: 12 hours and 15 minutes
Cooking Time: 2 hours and 30 minutes
Servings: 4

Ingredients:

- 1/3 cup olive oil
- 6 cloves garlic
- 3 tablespoons fresh thyme
- 3 tablespoons fresh rosemary
- Pinch steak seasoning
- 7 lb. prime rib roast

Method:

1. Add the olive oil, garlic, herbs and seasoning in a food processor.
2. Pulse until smooth.
3. Coat the prime rib with the paste.
4. Cover and refrigerate for 12 hours.
5. Preheat your Pit Boss Grill to 250 degrees F.
6. Grill the prime rib for 2 hours.
7. Increase temperature to 400 degrees F.
8. Grill for 15 to 30 minutes.

Serving Suggestions: Serve with mashed potatoes and mushroom gravy.

Preparation & Cooking Tips: You can also try searing the steak after roasting for 1 to 2 minutes over high flame to get a crunchier crust.

Beef Kefta

Preparation Time: 1 hour and 10 minutes

Cooking Time: 10 minutes

Servings: 4

Ingredients:

- 1 onion, grated
- 2 lb. ground beef
- 1 tablespoon blackened saskatchewan rub seasoning
- 3 tablespoon cilantro, chopped
- 1 teaspoon cumin
- 1 teaspoon paprika
- 3 tablespoon parsley, chopped

Method:

1. Combine all the ingredients in a bowl.
2. Mix well.
3. Refrigerate for 1 hour.
4. Set your Pit Boss Grill to smoke.
5. Preheat it to 425 degrees F or medium high heat.
6. Shape the beef mixture into cylinders.
7. Grill the beef kefta for 5 minutes per side.

Serving Suggestions: Serve with tzatziki sauce and pita bread.

Preparation & Cooking Tips: Marinate overnight for more intense flavors.

Coffee Steak

Preparation Time: 15 minutes
Cooking Time: 35 minutes
Servings: 8

Ingredients:

- Garlic salt to taste
- Pinch instant coffee
- 4 rib eye steaks

Method:

1. Rub garlic salt and coffee on both sides of steaks.
2. Set your Pit Boss Grill to smoke.
3. Preheat your grill to 350 degrees F.
4. Add the steaks to the grill.
5. Smoke the steaks for 30 minutes.
6. Increase temperature to 375 degrees F.
7. Grill the steaks for 5 minutes.

Serving Suggestions: Pair with buttered vegetables.

Preparation & Cooking Tips: Use freshly ground coffee.

Beef Caldereta Stew

Preparation Time: 40 minutes
Cooking Time: 1 hour and 30 minutes
Servings: 12

Ingredients:

- 2 tablespoons olive oil
- 2 lb. beef chuck roast, sliced into cubes
- Salt to taste
- 4 cloves garlic, chopped
- 2 red bell peppers, sliced
- 2 green bell peppers, sliced
- 2 potatoes, diced
- 2 tablespoons tomato paste
- 2 cups tomato sauce
- 2 cups water
- ½ cup cheddar cheese, grated

Method:

1. Preheat your Pit Boss Grill to 375 degrees F.
2. Add a cast iron pan on top of your grill.
3. Pour the oil into the pan.
4. Add the beef and cook until browned.
5. Season with salt.
6. Stir in the vegetables.
7. Cook while stirring for 5 minutes.
8. Add the tomato paste, tomato sauce and water.
9. Bring to a boil.
10. Reduce temperature to 275 degrees F.

11. Simmer for 1 hour.
12. Top with the cheese.
13. Cook for 2 more minutes and serve.

Serving Suggestions: Serve with hot cooked rice.

Preparation & Cooking Tips: Smoke the vegetables first before adding to the stew.

Beef Shawarma

Preparation Time: 1 hour and 10 minutes

Cooking Time: 10 minutes

Servings: 4

Ingredients:

- 1 ½ lbs flank steak
- 2 teaspoon olive oil
- 2 cloves garlic, minced
- 1 teaspoon paprika
- 1 ½ teaspoon ground coriander
- ½ teaspoon cayenne pepper
- ½ teaspoon ground cloves
- ½ teaspoon ground cinnamon

Method:

1. Combine all the ingredients in a bowl.
2. Mix well.
3. Cover and refrigerate for 1 hour.
4. Preheat your Pit Boss Grill to 450 degrees F.
5. Grill the steaks for 5 minutes per side.
6. Transfer to a cutting board.
7. Slice across the grain.

Serving Suggestions: Serve with pita bread and toppings of your choice.

Preparation & Cooking Tips: You can also use skirt steak or hanger steak for this recipe.

Korean Barbecue Short Ribs

Preparation Time: 1 hour and 15 minutes
Cooking Time: 4 hours
Servings: 4

Ingredients:

- ½ cup soy sauce
- 1 cup beef broth
- 1 tablespoon beef & brisket rub
- 1 tablespoon ginger, grated
- 3 cloves garlic, peeled
- 2 tablespoon brown sugar
- 4 beef short ribs
- 1 tablespoon sriracha sauce
- Toasted sesame seeds

Method:

1. Mix soy sauce, broth, rub, ginger, garlic and sugar in a bowl.
2. Transfer to a sealable plastic.
3. Stir in the short ribs.
4. Marinate in the refrigerator for 1 hour.
5. Preheat your Pit Boss Grill to 250 degrees F.
6. Grill the ribs for 4 hours, turning several times.
7. Sprinkle with sesame seeds and serve.

Serving Suggestions: Serve with rice and kimchi.

Preparation & Cooking Tips: You can also marinate for longer hours.

Grilled Tomahawk Steak

Preparation Time: 1 hour and 20 minutes
Cooking Time: 45 minutes
Servings: 2

Ingredients:

- 2 tomahawk rib eye steaks
- Salt to taste
- 2 tablespoons steak seasoning
- 3 tablespoons butter
- 2 cloves garlic, minced
- 1 sprig rosemary, minced

Method:

1. Preheat your Pit Boss Grill to 225 degrees F.
2. Season the steak with salt.
3. Let sit for 1 hour.
4. Seasons the steak with the steak seasoning.
5. Grill the steak for 45 minutes, turning once.
6. In a bowl, mix the butter, garlic and rosemary.
7. Top steak with the garlic butter and serve.

Serving Suggestions: Let steak rest for 10 minutes before serving.

Preparation & Cooking Tips: Use bone-in tomahawk steak for this recipe.

Steak Tips

Preparation Time: 15 minutes
Cooking Time: 15 minutes
Servings: 4

Ingredients:

- 2 lb. strip sirloin steak
- 4 tablespoons steak seasoning
- ¼ cup butter
- 1 tablespoon garlic, minced

Method:

1. Season the steaks with the steak seasoning.
2. Preheat your Pit Boss Grill to 375 degrees F.
3. Grill the steaks for 5 to 7 minutes per side.
4. Transfer to a cutting board and slice into strips.
5. In a pan over medium heat, melt the butter and cook the garlic until fragrant.
6. Drizzle steak tips with butter sauce.

Serving Suggestions: Serve with cooked mashed potatoes.

Preparation & Cooking Tips: Marinate steak in broth overnight.

Mustard Prime Rib Roast

Preparation Time: 15 minutes

Cooking Time: 3 hours and 5 minutes

Servings: 8

Ingredients:

- 1 cup mustard
- 2 tablespoons garlic, minced
- 1 tablespoon salt
- 1 tablespoon pepper
- 1 prime rib roast

Method:

1. Preheat your Pit Boss Grill to 450 degrees F.
2. Mix the mustard, garlic, salt and pepper in a bowl.
3. Rub the roast with the mixture.
4. Place the roast on top of the grill.
5. Cover the grill.
6. Cook for 45 minutes.
7. Reduce temperature to 325 degrees F.
8. Cook for another 2 hours and 30 minutes.

Serving Suggestions: Let rest for 15 minutes before slicing and serving.

Preparation & Cooking Tips: Use whole grain mustard for this recipe.

Chapter 6: Vegetable Recipes

Green Chili Mashed Potatoes

Preparation Time: 20 minutes
Cooking Time: 40 minutes
Servings: 4

Ingredients:

- 3 lb. potatoes, sliced in half
- Water
- ½ cup green chili
- ½ cup butter
- Pinch smoked rub
- ¼ milk
- 2 tablespoons smoked seasoning

Method:

1. Boil the potatoes in a pot with water.
2. Cook until tender.
3. Drain the potatoes.
4. Preheat your Pit Boss Grill to 350 degrees F.
5. Add the potatoes on top of the grill.
6. Add the green chili beside the potatoes.
7. Cook for 10 minutes.
8. Transfer to a plate and let cool.
9. Transfer to a food processor along with the rest of the ingredients.
10. Process until smooth.

Serving Suggestions: Serve immediately.

Preparation & Cooking Tips: You can omit green chili if you don't like mashed potatoes spicy.

Cheesy Potato Casserole

Preparation Time: 15 minutes

Cooking Time: 1 hour and 30 minutes

Servings: 15

Ingredients:

- Cooking spray
- 32 oz. potatoes, sliced
- 1 can cream of mushroom soup
- 1 can cream of celery soup
- 1 1lb. cheese sauce
- 8 oz. sour cream
- Pinch steak seasoning

Method:

1. Preheat your Pit Boss Grill to 350 degrees F.
2. Spray your baking pan with oil.
3. Spread potatoes in the baking pan.
4. Mix the remaining ingredients in a bowl.
5. Top the potatoes with this mixture.
6. Cover with foil.
7. Cook on top of the grill for 1 hour.
8. Remove foil and cook for 30 more minutes.

Serving Suggestions: Let rest for 15 minutes before serving.

Preparation & Cooking Tips: Use low-fat sour cream.

Garlic Potatoes

Preparation Time: 10 minutes
Cooking Time: 30 minutes
Servings: 6

Ingredients:

- 4 red potatoes, sliced
- 3 tablespoons butter, melted
- 1 onion, sliced
- 3 cloves garlic, minced

Method:

1. Preheat your Pit Boss Grill to 400 degrees F.
2. Spread the potatoes in a baking pan.
3. Stir in the rest of the ingredients.
4. Cover the pan with foil.
5. Cook on the grill for 30 minutes or until tender.

Serving Suggestions: Sprinkle with chopped parsley before serving.

Preparation & Cooking Tips: You can also top with mozzarella or cheddar cheese.

Chili Verde Sauce

Preparation Time: 15 minutes
Cooking Time: 10 minutes
Servings: 4

Ingredients:

- 1 onion, sliced
- 3 cloves garlic, peeled
- 4 serrano chili pepper
- 1 lb. tomatillos, husked
- ¼ cup olive oil, divided
- 1 tablespoon sweet heat rub
- 1 cup cilantro

Method:

1. Drizzle the onion, garlic, chili pepper and tomatillos with 2 tablespoons olive oil.
2. Set the Pit Boss Grill to 375 degrees F.
3. Grill for 5 to 10 minutes.
4. Transfer to a plate and let cool.
5. Add grilled veggies to a food processor along with the remaining ingredients.
6. Process until smooth.

Serving Suggestions: Serve with pita chips.

Preparation & Cooking Tips: Use apple hardwood pellets for this recipe.

Mexican Corn Salad

Preparation Time: 10 minutes
Cooking Time: 10 minutes
Servings: 4

Ingredients:

- 1 tablespoon cilantro, chopped
- 4 cobs corn
- 1 tablespoon lime juice
- 1 tablespoon chicken seasoning
- 1 teaspoon paprika
- ¼ cup sour cream
- 2 tablespoon mayo
- ½ cup feta cheese, crumbled

Method:

1. Preheat your Pit Boss Grill to 350 degrees F.
2. Grill the corn for 10 minutes, turning several times.
3. Slice off the corn kernels and add to a bowl.
4. Stir in the rest of the ingredients.

Serving Suggestions: Serve immediately.

Preparation & Cooking Tips: Use smoked paprika.

Mashed Potato Cakes

Preparation Time: 40 minutes
Cooking Time: 10 minutes
Servings: 6

Ingredients:

- 3 cups mashed potatoes
- ½ cup bacon bits, cooked
- 1 egg, beaten
- 1 cup cheddar jack cheese, shredded
- 1 teaspoon hickory bacon rub
- 1/3 cup flour
- 4 scallions, minced
- 2 tablespoons butter
- 2 teaspoons mustard

Method:

1. Combine all the ingredients in a bowl.
2. Form balls from the mixture.
3. Flatten the balls to form the patties.
4. Add the potato cakes on top of the grill.
5. Cook over medium low heat for 3 minutes per side or until golden.

Serving Suggestions: Sprinkle with chopped scallions.

Preparation & Cooking Tips: You can also use spicy mustard.

Grilled Cauliflower Salad

Preparation Time: 15 minutes

Cooking Time: 10 minutes

Servings: 6

Ingredients:

- 1 head cauliflower, sliced into 4 portions
- 1 tablespoon olive oil
- 1 cup mayonnaise
- 1 cup sour cream
- 2 tablespoons brown mustard
- 8 hard-boiled eggs, peeled and sliced
- ½ cup bacon, cooked and crumbled
- ¼ cup parsley, chopped
- 3 scallions, chopped
- Garlic salt to taste

Method:

1. Drizzle cauliflower with olive oil.
2. Preheat your Pit Boss Grill to 375 degrees F.
3. Grill the cauliflower for 5 minutes per side.
4. Separate into florets and place in a bowl.
5. Stir in the rest of the ingredients.

Serving Suggestions: Refrigerate for 30 minutes before serving.

Preparation & Cooking Tips: Stir gently so that the eggs won't be crushed.

Grilled Pickles with Bacon

Preparation Time: 10 minutes
Cooking Time: 45 minutes
Servings: 6

Ingredients:

- 13 strips bacon
- 13 spears dill pickles

Method:

1. Preheat your Pit Boss Grill to 375 degrees F.
2. Wrap the dill pickles with the bacon.
3. Secure with a toothpick.
4. Grill for 45 minutes, turning several times.

Serving Suggestions: Serve with a mix of sour cream and chopped chives.

Preparation & Cooking Tips: You can also sprinkle with steak seasoning before grilling.

Southern Green Beans

Preparation Time: 15 minutes
Cooking Time: 1 hour and 15 minutes
Servings: 6

Ingredients:

- 4 slices bacon
- 1 tablespoon butter
- 2 lb. green beans, trimmed
- 2 cups water
- 2 cups chicken broth
- Pinch hickory bacon seasoning

Method:

1. Preheat your Pit Boss Grill to 350 degrees F or medium heat.
2. Add a cast iron skillet on top of the grill.
3. Add the bacon and cook for 15 minutes.
4. Transfer the bacon to a plate.
5. Add the rest of the ingredients to the pan.
6. Close the grill lid.
7. Cook for 1 hour.
8. While waiting, chop the bacon.
9. Sprinkle chopped bacon on top of the green beans and serve.

Serving Suggestions: Serve with grilled steak.

Preparation & Cooking Tips: You can also add potato wedges to the dish.

Asparagus with Bacon

Preparation Time: 10 minutes
Cooking Time: 30 minutes
Servings: 4

Ingredients:

- 1 bunch asparagus
- Bacon slices

Method:

1. Preheat your Pit Boss Grill to 400 degrees F.
2. Wrap each asparagus spear with bacon slice.
3. Place on the grill.
4. Grill for 25 minutes, turning once or twice.

Serving Suggestions: Serve with hot sauce.

Preparation & Cooking Tips: You can also smoke the bacon before grilling.

Chapter 7: Vegetarian/Vegan Recipes

Cowboy Beans

Preparation Time: 10 minutes
Cooking Time: 3 hours
Servings: 8

Ingredients:

- 1 cup barbecue sauce
- 10 oz. canned diced tomatoes with green chili
- 6 cloves garlic, minced
- 2 jalapeno peppers, chopped
- Salt to taste
- 1 lb. pinto beans, dried
- 1 tablespoon Worcestershire sauce
- 1 yellow onion, chopped
- Water

Method:

1. Preheat your Pit Boss Grill to 400 degrees F or medium high heat.
2. Add all the ingredients to your Dutch oven and place it on top of the grill.
3. Bring to a boil.
4. Cover the pot and reduce temperature to 300 degrees F.
5. Cook for 1 hour.
6. Reduce temperature to 275 degrees F and cook for 2 hours.

Serving Suggestions: Serve with crusty bread.

Preparation & Cooking Tips: Be sure to rinse beans thoroughly before preparing.

Sweet Potato Casserole

Preparation Time: 10 minutes

Cooking Time: 1 hour and 30 minutes

Servings: 4

Ingredients:

- ¼ cup brown sugar
- ¼ cup vegan butter
- 4 oz. pecans, chopped
- ½ teaspoon cinnamon
- 2 teaspoons apple butter rub
- 4 sweet potatoes, sliced

Method:

1. Preheat your Pit Boss Grill to 350 degrees F or medium high heat.
2. Combine all the ingredients in a baking pan.
3. Cover the pan with foil.
4. Add to the grill.
5. Cook for 1 hour.
6. Increase temperature to 375 degrees F.
7. Cook for another 30 minutes.

Serving Suggestions: Sprinkle with ground cinnamon before serving.

Preparation & Cooking Tips: You can also use butternut squash for this recipe.

Sweet Potato Medley

Preparation Time: 15 minutes
Cooking Time: 45 minutes
Servings: 8

Ingredients:

- 8 Brussels sprouts, sliced in half
- 2 sweet potatoes, diced
- 3 tablespoons olive oil
- ½ white onion, sliced
- 1 red bell pepper, sliced
- Lemon pepper seasoning

Method:

1. Toss the ingredients in a baking pan.
2. Cover with foil.
3. Add to the grill.
4. Set your Pit Boss Grill to 450 degrees F.
5. Cook for 45 minutes, stirring once.

Serving Suggestions: Sprinkle with lemon pepper seasoning before serving.

Preparation & Cooking Tips: You can add more vegetables if you like.

Grilled Zucchini

Preparation Time: 10 minutes

Cooking Time: 30 minutes

Servings: 4

Ingredients:

- 2 zucchinis, sliced in half lengthwise
- Olive oil
- Pinch garlic salt

Method:

1. Drizzle zucchini with olive oil.
2. Season with garlic salt.
3. Add to the Pit Boss Grill.
4. Set the grill to 375 degrees F.
5. Grill for 10 to 15 minutes per side.

Serving Suggestions: Top with fresh tomato salsa before serving.

Preparation & Cooking Tips: You can also season with pepper.

Corn with Cilantro & Lime

Preparation Time: 10 minutes

Cooking Time: 20 minutes

Servings: 4

Ingredients:

- 2 tablespoons butter, melted
- ½ cup cilantro, chopped
- 4 cobs corn
- 2 tablespoons lime juice

Method:

1. Preheat your Pit Boss grill to 400 degrees F.
2. Grill the corn for 15 minutes, rotating often.
3. Brush the corn with butter.
4. Sprinkle with the cilantro and drizzle with lime juice.

Serving Suggestions: You can also slice the corn into 3 portions before serving.

Preparation & Cooking Tips: You can also add paprika if you like it spicy.

Tofu & Vegetable Kebab

Preparation Time: 15 minutes
Cooking Time: 15 minutes
Servings: 4

Ingredients:

- 1 block tofu, sliced into cubes
- 1 white onion, sliced
- 1 red bell pepper, sliced
- 1 green bell pepper, sliced
- Olive oil
- ¼ teaspoon cumin
- ½ teaspoon garlic powder

Method:

1. Preheat your Pit Boss Grill to 350 degrees F.
2. Thread tofu and vegetables alternately onto skewers.
3. Drizzle with oil and season with cumin and garlic powder.
4. Grill for 10 to 15 minutes, rotating frequently.

Serving Suggestions: Serve with garlic sauce.

Preparation & Cooking Tips: Use extra firm tofu.

Lemon Garlic Tofu

Preparation Time: 10 minutes

Cooking Time: 10 minutes

Servings: 4

Ingredients:

- 1 block tofu, sliced
- 1 tablespoon olive oil
- 1 tablespoon lemon juice
- 1 teaspoon garlic powder
- Pepper to taste

Method:

1. Drizzle tofu with a mix of olive oil and lemon juice.
2. Sprinkle with garlic powder and pepper.
3. Place on the Pit Boss Grill.
4. Set it to 375 degrees F.
5. Grill for 5 minutes per side.

Serving Suggestions: Serve with dip of choice.

Preparation & Cooking Tips: Use extra-firm tofu for this recipe.

Roasted Bell Peppers

Preparation Time: 10 minutes

Cooking Time: 10 minutes

Servings: 4

Ingredients:

- 1 red bell pepper, sliced in half
- 1 yellow bell pepper, sliced in half
- 1 green bell pepper, sliced in half
- 1 orange bell pepper, sliced in half
- Olive oil
- Salt and pepper to taste

Method:

1. Preheat your Pit Boss Grill to 350 degrees F.
2. Drizzle bell peppers with oil.
3. Season with salt and pepper.
4. Add to the grill.
5. Grill for 3 to 5 minutes per side.

Serving Suggestions: Serve as side dish to grilled main course.

Preparation & Cooking Tips: Use large bell peppers.

Lemon Garlic Green Beans

Preparation Time: 10 minutes

Cooking Time: 20 minutes

Servings: 6

Ingredients:

- 1 lb. green beans, trimmed
- 5 tablespoons butter, melted
- 3 cloves garlic, minced
- Pepper to taste
- Pinch lemon pepper garlic seasoning

Method:

1. Set your Pit Boss Grill to smoke.
2. Preheat it to 350 degrees F.
3. Toss all ingredients in a baking pan.
4. Cover pan with foil.
5. Place the pan on top of the grill.
6. Grill for 20 minutes.

Serving Suggestions: Sprinkle with crispy garlic bits.

Preparation & Cooking Tips: Use vegan butter or olive oil to make this vegetarian recipe vegan.

Grilled Mushrooms

Preparation Time: 10 minutes
Cooking Time: 15 minutes
Servings: 4

Ingredients:

- 4 large Portobello mushrooms
- 1 tablespoon olive oil
- 1 teaspoon garlic salt
- 2 tablespoons parsley, chopped

Method:

1. Drizzle mushrooms with oil.
2. Sprinkle with garlic salt.
3. Set your Pit Boss Grill to 375 degrees F.
4. Cook for 15 minutes, turning twice.
5. Sprinkle with parsley before serving.

Serving Suggestions: Serve with dip of choice.

Preparation & Cooking Tips: You can also use garlic powder for this recipe.

Conclusion

It is hard to find anyone who does not like grilled food. The rich, savory, and smoky flavors are just irresistible and appetizing. Wood pellet grills are great options if you love grilled food but hate using traditional wood or charcoal. Pellet grills are highly versatile appliances that are also user-friendly, providing you with diverse cooking options.

Pit Boss is now one of the most popular brands when it comes to grills and smokers. They offer the best value for money without skimping on quality. Pit Boss offers a variety of pellet grill configurations to match your requirements and budget.

Have fun experimenting with the many wood pellet flavors and use them to compliment all the exquisite recipes this cookbook has to offer. Whether you are a beginner or a seasoned cook, the many functions of a pellet grill will easily satisfy your culinary needs.

CPSIA information can be obtained
at www.ICGtesting.com
Printed in the USA
BVHW011155161121
621766BV00009B/203